Insight Into The 10 Ministries
of
The Nation of Islam

Civic Engagement

An Introduction To A Study of Government

By Abdul Wahid Muhammad

and

Rasheed L. Muhammad

Forward

The Muslim book of scripture speaks about demanding rights between men and women [mates] as one of the duties we must keep to Allah (God). This particular chapter is entitled, "The Women". Chapter 4 verse 1 says, *"O people, keep your duty to your Lord, Who created you from a single being and created its mate of the same (kind), and spread from these two many men and women. And keep your duty to Allah, by Whom **you demand one of another (your rights), and (to) the ties of relationship**. Surely Allah is ever a Watcher over you."*

In all our relationships, think about the Originator of the heavens and earth as *The Self-Created* single cell of life (God) splitting into two life cells ultimately producing mates as in a husband and wife. Can we say the basis of civics begin with the demands of rights made by husband and wife that set the character for all civic engagement, human rights and government systems?

What does demand mean. Demand means:

1. *(v. t.)* The asking or seeking for what is due or claimed as due.
2. *(v. t.)* A thing or amount claimed to be due.
3. *(v. t.)* The act of demanding; an asking with authority; a peremptory urging of a claim; a claiming or challenging as due; requisition; as, the demand of a creditor; a note payable on demand.
4. *(v. t.)* The right or title in virtue of which anything may be claimed; as, to hold a demand against a person.
5. *(v. t.)* A diligent seeking or search; manifested want; desire to possess; request; as, a demand for certain goods; a persons company is in great demand.
6. *(v. t.)* To require as necessary or useful; to be in urgent need of; hence, to call for; as, the case demands care.
7. *(v. t.)* To ask or call for with authority; to claim or seek from, as by authority or right; to claim, as something due; to call for urgently or peremptorily; as, to demand a debt; to demand obedience.

8. *(v. i.)* To make a demand; to inquire.
9. *(v. t.)* To call into court; to summon.
10. *(v. t.)* That which one demands or has a right to demand; thing claimed as due; claim; as, demands on an estate.
11. *(v. t.)* Earnest inquiry; question; query.
12. *(v. t.)* To inquire authoritatively or earnestly; to ask, esp. in a peremptory manner; to question.

To prolong human life and civilization, demands must be properly made to establish a vast network of agreements that maintains our ties with our descendants by means of duty, moral or civic obligation to experience a civil society. To succeed with such bonds resembling actions set out by *The Originator,* a portion of this booklet will entail how the pattern of the universe is after the pattern of God (The Originator of Self).

Furthermore, it is our belief that a real study of government and all its parts necessitate how God interacts with His own creation in an arranged manner full of guidance that must be measured and agreed upon. Each part being guided and directed with the wherewithal to demand its right to fulfill its purpose in creation. You ask but how? To begin with, the Honorable Minister Louis Farrakhan stated:

"After He created Himself, then came our universe. So the pattern of the universe is after the pattern of Himself. So if you want to study government, study how God made you...The solution is to model the government after the human body...created in Gods image.

"If we study this magnificent body … we can relate all these 10 systems to 10 ministries with subgroups and tasks forces that will allow us the privilege of building our own communities."[1]

Rasheed L. Muhammad - Abdul Wahid Muhammad

7/22/2017

---

[1] Holy Day of Atonement 2009 Accepting Responsibility to Build Our Community --Minister Louis Farrakhan Muhammad--

Work Booklet Syllabus

Assignment One: Listen to entire lecture of Minister Louis Farrakhan's 2009 Holy Day of Atonement Lecture ***"Accepting Responsibility to Build Our Community"***: Attain 9 names of the Nation of Islam's Executive Council as your first civic engagement assignment. [Pages 7-9]

Assignment Two: Civic Engagement: Nation: Foundation of Society: Land of Our Own: State: Territory: Rights: Duty: Citizenship: Government. ***Read each topic and answer all questions contained in these assignments***: [10-17]

What the Muslim Want: Early Pioneers of the Nation of Islam 1930 – 1940: Question and Answer to why no. 9. ***Answer all questions contained in these assignments.*** [Pages 18-23]

10 Ministries and Community Governance: Father of Economic Theory. Read each of the 10 Ministry analogies and their functionality in the Human Body's 10 Systems. ***Answer all questions contained in these assignments.*** [Pages 25-60]

Mixed Use Development: Failed State: ***Answer all questions contained in these assignments.*** [Pages 61-64]

Recommended Reading: *A Torchlight For America*, By Minister Louis Farrakhan, Your Brain and 9 Systems: Equal the Physio-Economics of God Divine Knowledge of God-Self by A. Wahid Muhammad and Rasheed L. Muhammad [Page 65]

Seminar Contact Information. [Page 66]

Muhammad Speaks Newspaper Pre-1975

Assignment One

All governance principles are rooted in the Holy Quran 22:41. A proper understanding of this verse, in principle, can guide national leaders and citizens to formulate and maintain good government, just laws and realistic engagement. Principally, it will serve as the underlining principles for all socio-economic and political objectives.

Instructions: Read the Quranic verse below and make the above statement true or false. If you answer is true explain. It false, explain.

[AND THEY ARE] THOSE WHO, IF WE GIVE THEM AUTHORITY IN THE LAND, ESTABLISH PRAYER AND GIVE ZAKAH AND ENJOIN WHAT IS RIGHT AND FORBID WHAT IS WRONG. AND TO ALLAH BELONGS THE OUTCOME OF [ALL] MATTERS. (HOLY QURAN 22:41)

____

____

____

____

____

____

____

Accepting Responsibility to Build Our Community

-Minister Louis Farrakhan-

"If we study this magnificent body ... we can relate all these 10 systems to 10 ministries with subgroups and tasks forces that will allow us the privilege of building our own communities."

Holy Day of Atonement 2009 Accepting Responsibility to Build Our Community
--Minister Louis Farrakhan Muhammad--

A ministry is a governmental organization, headed by a minister, which is usually meant to manage a specific sector of public administration. Ministries are usually an immediate subdivision of the Cabinet (i.e. an executive council), and subordinate to its chief executive also called chief minister.

Name 9 members of the Nation of Islam executive council, what are their roles by you and what is your role by them in terms of governance and civic responsibilities according to Holy Quran 22:41?

1

2

3

4

5

6

7

8

9

Assignment Two

Civic Engagement means working to make a difference in the civic life of our communities and developing the combination of knowledge, skills, values and motivation to make that difference...

A morally and civically responsible individual recognizes himself or herself as a member of a larger social fabric and therefore considers social problems to be at least partly his or her own; such an individual is willing to see the moral and civic dimensions of issues, to make and justify informed moral and civic judgments, and to take action when appropriate. [Source: *Civic Responsibility and Higher Education*, edited by Thomas Ehrlich, published by Oryx Press, 2000]

Nation is a large aggregate of people united by common descent, history, culture, or language, inhabiting a particular country or territory: [Source Bing.com]

Foundation of Society is based on a vast network of mutual agreements. What is it that compels people to abide by mutual agreements? For example, 1. Why stop at red lights? 2. Why demand rights from one another as male and female? 3. How can some people engineer people's behavior patterns and actions to become most cooperative in a free society?

What nation do you claim as your own? Explain by using the 3 above definitions.

____

____

____

____

____

____

____

____

1____

____

____

____

2____

____

____

____

3____

____

____

____

____

____

____

____

____

Land of Our Own: "We want our people in America whose parents or grandparents were descendants from slaves, to be allowed to establish a separate state or territory of their own - either on this continent or elsewhere. We believe that our former slave masters are obligated to provide such land and that the area must be fertile and minerally rich.

"We believe that our former slave masters are obligated to maintain and supply our needs in this separate territory for the next 20 to 25 years--until we are able to produce and supply our own needs. Since we cannot get along with them in peace and equality, after giving them 400 years of our sweat and blood and receiving in return some of the worst treatment human beings have ever experienced. We believe our contributions to this land and the suffering forced upon us by white America justifies our demand for complete separation in a state or territory of our own. [Source Point No. 4, What the Muslims Want]

State: The term means a people permanently occupying a fixed territory bound together by common habits and custom into one body politic exercising, through the medium of an organized government, independent sovereignty and control over all persons and things within its boundaries, capable of making war and peace and of entering into international relations with other states. [Source: Legal Dictionary]

Territory: The term *territory* has various meanings in different contexts. Generally, the term refers to a particular or indeterminate geographical area. In a legal context, territory usually denotes a geographical area that has been acquired by a particular country but has not been recognized as a full participant in that country's affairs. In the United States, Guam is one example of a territory. Though it is considered a part of the United States and is governed by the U.S. Congress, Guam does not have full rights of statehood, such as full representation in Congress or full coverage under the U.S. Constitution. [Source: Legal Dictionary]

Explain why members of the Nation of Islam are a nation.

____

____

____

____

____

____

What is a state? Can black people attain a land of their own?

____

____

____

____

____

____

____

____

____

____

____

____

Rights: A social agreement to structure the form of government, the content of laws, and the shape of morality as it is perceived. So what are Rights? What, extensionally, is the meaning of the word "my" in such expressions as…"my book". "my" automobile? A check changes hands and "your" automobile becomes "mine", but no changes results in the automobile. What has changed"…The changes is, of course, in the social agreements covering our behavior toward the automobile…The meaning of "yours" and mine….lies in how we intent to act…when society as a whole recognizes my "right of ownership",…it agrees to protect me in my intentions to (exercise my rights)…Society makes this agreement with me in return for my obeying its laws and paying my share of the expenses of government. [Source: Language in Thought and Actions by Samuel Ichiye Hayakawa]

Duty: *A legal obligation that entails mandatory conduct or performance.*

With respect to the laws relating to **Customs & Duties**, a tax owed to the government for the import or export of goods.

Read Holy Quran Chapter 4, explain how some of its aspects serve as a basis for human rights?

____

____

____

____

____

____

____

____

____

____

____

____

____

____

____

____

____

____

Citizenship is the status of a person recognized under the custom or law as being a legal member of a sovereign state. A person may have multiple citizenships and a person who does not have citizenship of any state is said to be stateless…Each country has its own policies, regulations and criteria as to who is entitled to its citizenship. A person can be recognized or granted citizenship on a number of basis. [Source: Wikipedia]

A Government is the system by which a state or community is controlled. In the Commonwealth of Nations, the word government is also used more narrowly to refer to the collective group of people that exercises executive authority in a state. This usage is analogous to what is called an "administration" in American English. [Source: Wikipedia]

To be a citizen of the United States of America, one has to take a civics test and therefore to pass the test you must study the history of the country because test question may range from:

a) When was the Constitution written?
b) Name one American Indian tribe in the United States.
c) *What is one promise you make when you become a United States citizen?

The answer to "c" is:

- ✓ give up loyalty to other countries
- ✓ defend the Constitution and laws of the United States
- ✓ obey the laws of the United States
- ✓ serve in the U.S. military (if needed)
- ✓ serve (do important work for) the nation (if needed)
- ✓ be loyal to the United States

When was the Muhammad Mosque Provisional Constitution of the Lost and Found Nation of Islam in West written, who wrote it, how many articles, what does it mean? What must a citizen learn about his or her government?

Some Early Pioneers of the Lost and Found Nation of Islam in the West 1930's to 1940's

(first row L-R) Minister Isaiah Karriem, Bro. Clarence, Bro. Elmer, Minister Sultan Muhammad, Minister James Shabazz, Minister Benjamin Muhammad and Bro. Jake. (second row) Bro. Charles X Worthington, Bro. Richard, Bro. John, Bro. Herbert, and other NOI Pioneers of Washington, D.C.

I AM
Baroness Sharrieff Mohammed
Reformer and Secretary
TO
MASTER W.D.F. MOHAMMED.
...and these are some
of my experiences

Instructions: Provide nineteen names of the Early Pioneers in the pictures whom you have heard about in our history books.

1____

2____

3____

4____

5____

6____

7____

8____

9____

10____

11____

12____

13____

14____

15____

16____

17____

18____

19____

Why did these early pioneers of the Nation of Islam consent to be governed under its Finder, Master Fard Muhammad, (W.D. Fard)?

____

____

____

____

____

____

____

____

What does the middle initial "D" mean in W.D. Fard (Master Fard Muhammad), finder of the Lost and Found Member of the Nation of Islam in the West?

The following question and answer was provided by Sister Burnsteen Sharrieff, the first female secretary to Master Fard Muhammad,. Her words about *9 Laborers* of the Nation of Islam working under *1 God* were made in 1948 to the women of Islam. So what we see here are 10 systems of government designed for the laborers or servants or Ministries of the N.O.I. to work out a plan of salvation.

Why nine?

Answer: The Supreme Court has 9 Judges, like our form 9 Laborers, all with original names. Why? To give you justice he must first have his own Title....

There are 9 great major planets, and the Sun rules them all...Allah have 9 laborers and he rules them all including his Servant Prophet Elijah Mohammed. [**Source:** A Summary of the Flag Demonstration Given to the M.G.T. & G.C.C By Captain Burnsteen Sharrieff Thursday May 20th, 1948 from the booklet, *"Warning & Instructions To The M.G.T. & G.C.C. from Elijah Mohammed: Mothers of the Faithful, Soldiers For Muhammad 1930's – 1940's*]

Image of 1 sun ruling all 9 planets

The next section of this book deals with Public Policy. **Policies** and procedures play a very important role by defining an organization's (community/nation) guiding principles, providing detailed task instructions and forming the basic structure of its business operations as well as setting in motion mutual agreements amongst the citizenry. Without public policy, the horde shall rule, might makes right and the tender mother is destroyed.

10 Ministries

Of

Community Governance

Instructions: Read each of the 10 Ministry analogies with the 9 human *involuntary* systems on the following pages. Write your own thoughts about what you can perceive therein, analogously. Then write a policy recommendation that you want to see in such community governance. Your policy recommendation, *for each ministry*, must include at least 5 of the 7 Core Components.

Core Components:

Although the policy paper relies on your authority over the deep research that you have conducted on the issue or problem, you should also pay close attention to audience, the professional expectations and jargon of your targeted decision makers, and the structure and flow of your argument. Here are some general attributes that structure the analysis and argument for most policy papers:

• Define the problem or issue. Highlight the urgency and state significant findings for the problem based on the statistics. Objectivity is your priority, so resist the urge to exaggerating.

• Analyze—do not merely present—the statistics. Show how you arrived at the findings or recommendations through analysis of qualitative or quantitative statistics. Draw careful conclusions that make sense of the data and do not misrepresent it. Your data should be replicable.

• Summarize your findings or state [community] recommendations. Provide specific recommendations or findings in response to specific problems and avoid generalizations.

• Generate conditions for evaluating statistics. Explain the key assumptions and methodology underlying your analysis and prioritize the criteria you rely on to assess evidence.

• If you are producing recommendations, develop a theory of change, and analyze the options and tradeoffs or adjustments according to your methodology and assess their likelihood. What are the pros and cons? What is feasible? What are the predictable outcomes? Develop a logic model to gird your analysis and support your assertions with relevant data.

• Suggest next steps and the implications of the findings or recommendations. You may briefly address the feasibility or likelihood of next steps or explore the implications of your analysis.

• <u>Concentrate</u> the conclusions succinctly in a concluding section and remind the decision-maker of the big picture, the overall goal, the necessity of the investigation, or of the urgency for action. This answers the "Who cares?" question that reminds the reader of the value of the research and recommendations. If you are targeting a decision maker, you should reflect the decision-maker's primary concerns.[2]

---

[2] https://www-cdn.law.stanford.edu/wp-content/uploads/2015/04/White-Papers-Guidelines.pdf

1. The **<u>Ministry of the Spiritual Department</u>** affects our communities, institutions, subgroups and task forces in three basic ways i.e.; mentally, spiritually and morally.

2. The Brains **<u>Pineal Body</u>** secretes black melanin to influence body-cells in three basic ways by facilitating the transference of information to (a) bring together, (b) decompose, or (c) rearrange.

3. The Pineal Gland (body) contains a pattern for The Ministry of the Spiritual Department. Both synthesize (3 basic functions) into a coherent whole.

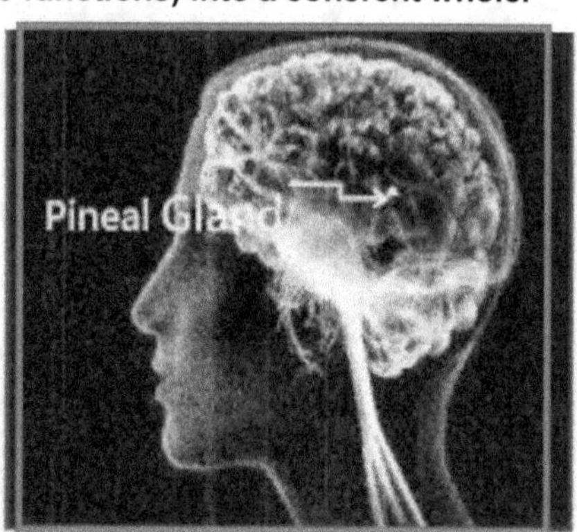

*The pineal gland synthesizes and secretes a black hormone called melatonin that communicates information about environmental conditions of the body to the mind's eye. Melatonin has the ability to entrain (transport by the flow of a fluid) biological rhythms and has important effects on reproductive function of [Humans]. The light-transducing ability of the pineal gland has led some to call the pineal the "third eye". Light exposure to the eyes dramatically affects the synthesis and secretion of melatonin.

Concentrations of melatonin increase ten-fold during sleep and then markedly decrease before awakening…Light exposure to the retina is first relayed to [the brains] hypothalamus, an area of the brain that coordinates biological clock signals.

Fibers from the hypothalamus descend to the spinal cord and ultimately....neurons ascend back to the pineal gland.[3]

What policy recommendations will help Spiritual Houses of worship fulfill its functionality to enlighten communities descending in darkness as the Pineal Body does for the environment of the human body?

____

____

____

____

____

____

____

____

____

____

____

____

____

____

____

[3] Source:www.vivo.colostate.edu/hbooks/pathphys/endocrine/otherendo/pineal.htm]

1. **The <u>Ministry of Science and Technology</u>** is upheld by mainframes built to house processing units for business transactions and vital information.

2. **The <u>Skeletal System</u> is the mainframe built to house sensitive organs** that enable transactions between vital life processes like lungs, brain, heart, etc.

3. The Skeletal System contains a pattern for the Ministry of Science and Technology. Both are mainframes that house and protect processing units and/or organs that enable us to conduct business.

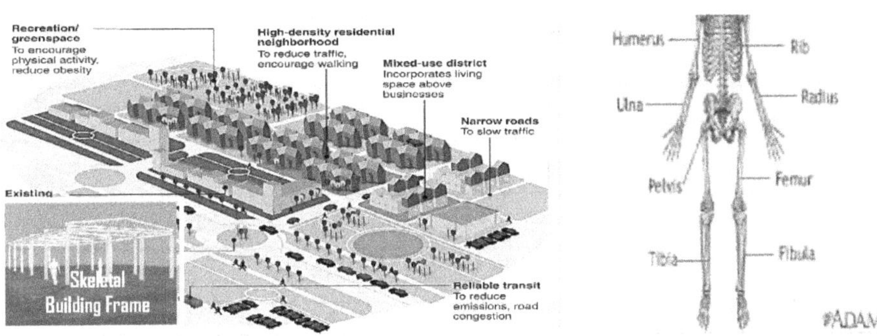

What policy recommendations will help the Ministry of Science and Technology fulfill its functionality as machine-pillars to uphold business processing activities for community vitality as the human skeletal system does for the organs of the human body?

____

____

____

____

____

____

1. **The <u>Ministry of Defense</u> is to defend in** three basic areas: a) community b) public property, c) business operations. A community is balanced with the proper strength that is demonstrated by public safety.

2. **Our <u>Muscle System</u>** represents strength in three distinct types of body muscles: (a) skeletal muscles, (b) heart muscles, and (c) smooth muscles found in the walls of hollow organs and blood vessels to force movement of fluids.

3. The Muscular System is exhibited by the outgrowth of the Ministry of Defense. Both function to provide protection, vitality and freedom of movement.

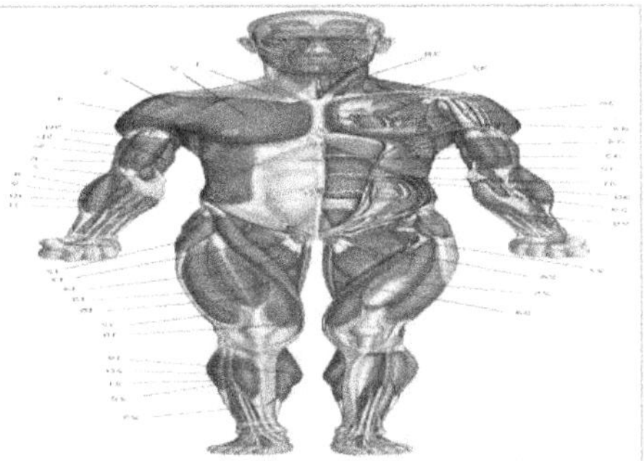

What policy recommendations will help Ministry of defense fulfill its functionality as the muscle strength needed to maintain public safety and free flow of citizenry's movement?

____

____

____

____

____

____

____

Father of Economic Theory

In his *Prolegomena (The Muqaddimah),* 'Abd al-Rahman Ibn Muhammad Ibn Khaldun al-Hadrami of Tunis (A.D. 1332-1406), commonly known as Ibn Khaldun, laid down the foundations of different fields of knowledge, in particular the science of civilization *(al-'umran).* His significant contributions to economics, however, should place him in the history of economic thought as a major forerunner, if not the "father," of economics, a title which has been given to Adam Smith, whose great works were published some three hundred and seventy years after Ibn Khaldun's deat..Ibn Khaldun was cognizant of these ideas, including the one relating to religious and moral perceptions. The relationship between moral and religious principles on one hand and good government on the other is effectively expounded in his citation and discussion of Tahir Ibn al-Husayn's (A.D. 775-822) famous letter to his son 'Abdallah, who ruled Khurasan with his descendants until A.D. 872.[1] From the rudimentary thoughts of Tahir[2] he developed a theory of taxation which has affected modern economic thought and even economic policies in the United States and elsewhere.

Not only did Ibn Khaldun plant the germinating seeds of classical economics, whether in production, supply, or cost, but he also pioneered in consumption, demand, and utility, the cornerstones of modern economic theory…

Who is Ibn Khaldun?

Labor Theory of Value, Economics of Labor, Labor as the Source of Growth and Capital Accumulation

According to Ibn Khaldun, labor is the source of value... Ibn Khaldun's contribution was later picked up by David Hume in his *Political Discourses,* published in 1752: "Everything in the world is purchased by labour."[7] This quotation was even used by Adam Smith as a footnote. "What is bought with money or with goods is purchased by labour, as much as what we acquire by the toil of our body. That money or those goods indeed save us this toil. They contain the value of a certain quantity of labour which we exchange for what is supposed at the time to contain the value of an equal quantity. The value of any commodity, therefore, to the person who possesses it, and who means not to use or consume it himself, but to exchange it for other commodities, is equal to the quantity of labour which it enables him to purchase or command. Labour, therefore, is the real measure of the exchangeable value of all commodities."[8] If this passage which was published in A.D. 1776 in Adam Smith's major work, is carefully analyzed, one can find its seeds in Ibn Khaldun's *Prolegomena (The Muqaddimah).* According to Ibn Khaldun, labor is the source of value. It is necessary for all earnings and capital accumulation. This is obvious in the case of craft. Even if earning "results from something other than a craft, the value of the resulting profit and acquired (capital) must (also) include the value of the labor by which it was obtained. Without labor, it would not have been acquired."[9]

Why are items bought with money or goods acquired by labor?

____

____

____

____

____

____

____

____

...His (Ibn Khaldun's) labor effort theory gave a reason for the rise of cities, which, as his insightful analysis of history indicated, were the focal points of civilizations...

Labor and its effort lead to production, which is in turn used for an exchange through barter or through the use of money, that is, gold and silver. The process therefore creates incomes and profits which a man derives from a craft as the value of his labor after having deducted the cost of raw material. Long before David Ricardo published his significant contribution to the field of economics in 1817, *The Principles of Political Economy and Taxation,* Ibn Khaldun gave the original explanation for the reasons behind the differences in labor earnings. They may be attributed to differences in skills, size of markets, location, craftsmanship or occupation, and the extent to which the ruler and his governors purchase the final product. As a certain type of labor becomes more precious, that is, if the demand for it exceeds its available supply, its earnings must rise.

High earnings in one craft attract others to it, a dynamic phenomenon which will eventually lead to an increase in its available supply and consequently lower profits. This principle explains Ibn Khaldun's original and insightful analysis of long-term adjustments within occupations and between one occupation and another. However, this point of view was attacked by John Maynard Keynes in his famous statement that in the long run we are all dead. Nevertheless, Ibn Khaldun's analysis has not only proved to be historically correct but has also constituted the core thinking of classical economists.[10]

What craft do you retain to enhance the labor force?

____

____

____

____

____

____

Ibn Khaldun succinctly observed, explained, and analyzed how earnings in one place may be different from another, even for the same profession. Earnings of judges, craftsmen, and even beggars, for example, are directly related to each town's degree of affluence and standard of living, which in themselves are to be achieved through the fruits of labor and the crystallization of productive communities...[12] It was Ibn Khaldun, not Adam Smith, who first presented the contribution of labor as a means of building up the wealth of a nation, stating that labor effort, increase in productivity, and exchange of products in large markets are the main reasons behind a country's wealth and prosperity. Inversely, a decline in productivity could lead to the deterioration of an economy and the earnings of its people. "A large civilization yields large profits [earnings] because of' the large amount of [available] labor which is the cause of [profit]."[13]

How does a civilization produce large profits?

____

____

____

____

____

To maximize both earnings and levels of satisfaction, a man should be free to perform whatever his gifted talents and skilled abilities dictate. Through natural talents and acquired skills, man can freely produce objects of' high quality, and, often, more units of labor per hour.

How will skilled laborers make a more prosperous civilization?

____

____

____

____

Demand, Supply, Prices, and Profits

In addition to his original contribution to the economics of labor, Ibn Khaldun introduced and ingeniously analyzed the interplay of several tools of economic analysis, such is demand, supply, prices, and profits.

Demand for an object is based on the utility of acquiring it and not necessarily the need for it. Utility is therefore the motive force behind demand. It creates the incentives for consumer spending in the marketplace...Similarly, if the demand for a certain craft decreases, its sales fall and consequently its price is reduced.

How is this above statement true or false?

____

____

____

Ibn Khaldun also made an original contribution in his concept of profits. In economic literature, a theory of profit as a reward for undertaking risk in a future of uncertainties is generally attributed to Frank Knight, who published his ideas in 1921.[18] There is no doubt that Frank Knight substantially advanced a well-established theory of profit. Nevertheless, it was Ibn Khaldun, not Frank Knight, who originally planted the seed of this theory: "Commerce means the buying of merchandise and goods, storing them, and waiting until fluctuation of the market brings about an increase in the prices of (these goods). _This is called profit (ribh)._"[19] In another context, Ibn Khaldun stated again the same idea: "Intelligent and experienced people in the cities know that it is inauspicious to hoard grain and to wait for high prices, and that the profit (expected) may be spoiled or lost through (hoarding)."[20] Profit is therefore a reward for undertaking a risk. In the face of future uncertainties, a risk-bearer may very well lose instead of gain. Similarly, profits or losses may accrue as a result of speculation which is carried out by profit-seekers in the marketplace.

How is commerce defined by Ibn Khaldun?

____

____

____

____

____

____

____

____

____

____

To maximize profits, Ibn Khaldun introduced a gospel for traders, "Buy cheap and sell dear,"[21]

...Nevertheless, Ibn Khaldun concluded that both excessively low prices and excessively high prices are disruptive to markets. It is therefore advisable that states not hold prices artificially low through subsidies or other methods of market intervention. Such **_policies_** are economically disastrous because the low-priced goods will disappear from the market and there will be no incentive for suppliers to produce and sell whenever their profits are adversely affected. Ibn Khaldun also concluded that excessively high prices will not be compatible with market expansion. As the high-priced goods sell less in the market, the policy of excessively high pricing becomes counterproductive and disrupts the flow of goods in markets...

What happens small rice farmers if the government buys more rice than the population is consuming? What happens to rice prices if the government hoards its rice for rainy day?

____

____

____

____

____

____

Ibn Khaldun's answer is: As a result, the expenditures of the inhabitants increase tremendously in proportion to the civilization of (the city). A great deal of money is spent. Under these circumstances, (people) need a great deal of money for expenditures, to procure the necessities of life for themselves and their families, as well as all other requirements.[21]

As to the impact of restricted supply on the price level, Ibn Khaldun summed it up thus: "When goods are few and rare, their prices go up."[24]

By carefully reading the above two passages, it becomes obvious that Ibn Khaldun discovered what is now known as cost-push and demand-pull causes of inflationary pressures.

Why are the prices of diamonds exceedingly high? How are the DeBeers?

Macroeconomics, Growth, Taxes, Role of Governments, and Money

In macroeconomics,…When there is more total demand as population increases, there is more production, profits, customs, and taxes. The upward cycle of growth continues as civilization flourishes and a new wave of total demand is created for the crafts and luxury products. "The value realized from them increases, and, as a result, profits are again *multiplied* in the town. Production there is thriving even more than before. And so it goes with the *second* and *third* increase."[26] People's "wealth, therefore, increases and their riches grow, the customs and ways of luxury *multiply*, and all the various kinds of crafts are firmly established among them."[27]

Modern national income accounts were also developed and expanded using the equality of income and expenditures. Expenditures of one citizen are income to others; therefore total expenditures are equal to total incomes. This equality was first discovered by Ibn Khaldun. In fact, he used both terms as synonymous to one another after having established the equality between them.[28] "Income and expenditure balance each other in every city. If the income is large, the expenditure is large, and vice versa. And if both income and expenditure are large, the inhabitants become more favourably situated, and the city grows."[29]

"I said (to them): 'ask forgiveness from your Lord; verily He is Oft-Forgiving. He will send rain to you in abundance; And give you increase in wealth and children, and bestow on you gardens and bestow on you rivers." Qur'an 71:10–12

How can you compare the above Quranic verse with the above two paragraphs?

____

____

____

____

(Man) obtains (some profits) through no efforts of his own, as, for instance, through rain that makes the fields thrive, and similar things. However, these things are only contributory. His own efforts must be combined with them, as will be mentioned. (His) profits will constitute his livelihood, if they correspond to his necessities and needs. They will be capital accumulation it they are greater than (his needs)."[30]

Governments play an important role in growth and in the country's economy in general through their purchases of goods and services and through their fiscal policy of taxation and expenditures. Governments may also provide an environment of incentives for work and prosperity or, inversely, a system of oppression which is ultimately self-defeating. Even though Ibn Khaldun regards governments as inefficient, "not so much calculation" is carried out by them of what is contemporarily known as cost and benefit, they still play an important role in the country's economy through their big purchases. Government expenditures stimulate the economy by increasing incomes, which are further hiked through a multiplier effect. However, if the king hoards the amount he collects in taxes, business slackens and the economic activities of the state are adversely affected through the multiplier effect.[31] In addition to its welfare program for the poor, the widows, the orphans, and the blind, provided there is no overburden for the treasury, the government should spend its tax revenue wisely to improve conditions of its "subjects, to safeguard their rights and to preserve them from harm."[32]

Read Holy Quran, Chapter 2 verse 177 and explain what it says concerning how to deal with the poor or wayfarer.

In macroeconomics Ibn Khaldun also contributed to the theory of money. According to him, money is not a real form of wealth but a vehicle through which it can be acquired. He was the first to present the major functions of money as a measure of value, a store of value and a "numeraire." "The two mineral 'stones,' gold and silver as the (measure of) value for all capital accumulations . . . [are] considered treasure and property. Even if under certain circumstances, other things are acquired, it only for the purpose of ultimately obtaining [them]. All other things are subject to market fluctuations from which (gold and silver) are exempt. ... Money also facilitates the flow of goods from one market to another, even across the border of countries.

What is the difference between paper money and (gold and silver)? How should both medians of exchange to be used by governments and citizens?

____

____

____

____

____

____

____

____

____

____

____

____

____

____

Ibn Khaldun defends a stable monetary policy. He is against the authorities playing with the value of currency. He fears that the authorities may be tempted to devalue the currency in order to build palaces and finance mercenary armies. This process will cause inflation and the population will lose confidence in the currency. These developments are considered to be unjust. As a supreme policy for the society, the protection of the purchasing power of money has to be implemented as a matter of justice. To do that, he proposed an independent monetary agency under the authority of Chief Justice, a "God-fearing man" to prevent the rulers "fearlessly" from tampering with the value of money and devaluing the currency. [**Source:** http://muslimheritage.com/article/economic-theory-ibn-khaldun-and-rise-and-fall-nations]

[Source:] http://faculty.georgetown.edu/imo3/ibn.htm

What is the importance of Economic order? How would you describe an independent monetary agency under the authority of a Chief Justice...?

____

____

____

1. **The Ministry of Trade and Commerce** entails a financial system for the distribution of resources and currency throughout the entire community. **In a healthy economy; currency must circulate several times before leaving**. Any other way means decay and death.

2. **Our Circulatory System** distributes blood, oxygen, currency and nutrients throughout the body to stimulate all its organs. Any other way means decay and death.

3. The Human Body produces 10--100 millimeters of currency – voltage.

This represents a pattern how and why Government currency is to be circulated.

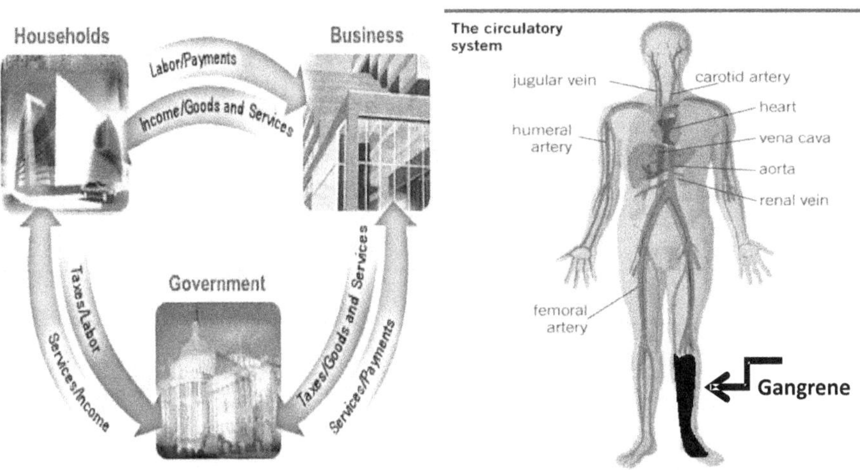

What policy recommendations will help the Ministry of Trade and Commerce fulfill its functionality as a financial apparatus to assure money circulation flows in and out of communities as the circulation system does for the human body?

____

____

____

____

____

1. **<u>The Ministry of Education</u> processes the knowledge we consume**. It is commonly broken down into stages. Education strengthens the mentality of a community toward productivity and growth.

2. **Our Digestive System processes food we consume.** It is where our body breaks down food into smaller parts. Food serves as strength and nourishment to keep the body productive and growing.

3. The Ministry of Education is patterned after the Digestive System. Both process and break down what we consume to balance our emotional state, growth, development and productivity.

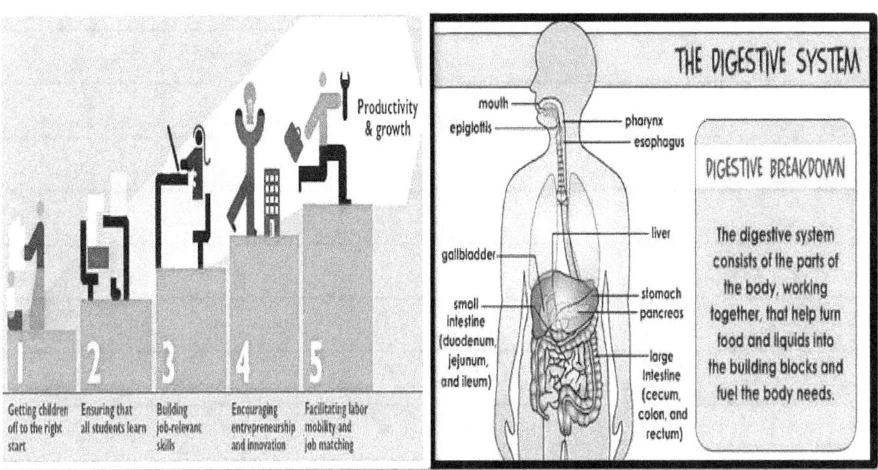

What policy recommendations will help the Ministry of Education to fulfill its functionality to assure communities receive, understand and digest healthy information to build communities, develop properly and fuel growth as the digestive system does for the human body?

____

____

____

____

____

1. **The _Ministry of Justice_ is a Law enforcement agency jurisdiction**. Law enforcement is a local defense system structured to protect community body-politics from persons of ill will and intentions.

2. **Our _Immune System_ is the body's defense system structured against infections** and outside germs that give negative feedback to the body politic. Generally, the immune system understands how to deal with germs.

3. The Ministry of Justice is patterned after the Immune System. One protects the entire human body, while the other protects the entire social order to preserve the community-body politic.

Immune System Nods

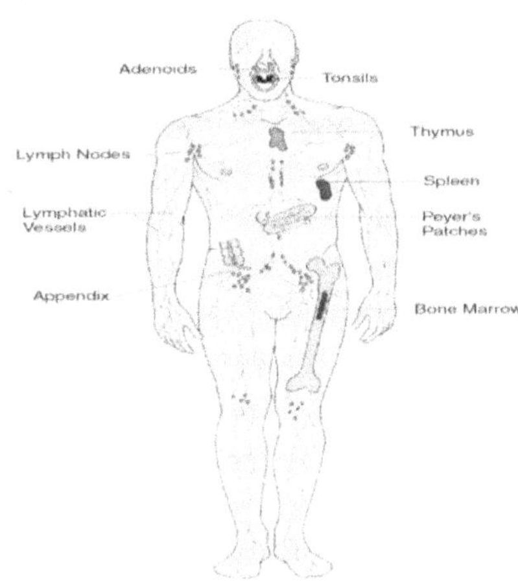

What policy recommendations will help the Ministry of Justice to fulfill its functionality to assure our entire society is protected from corruption, crime, and vice as the immune system does for the entire human body?

____

____

____

____

1. **The Ministry of Arts and Culture** renews **communities** by its concert halls, museums, libraries, theaters and studios; recreational infrastructure, tourism infrastructure, convention centers and amusement parks. **People pick up these activities to keep culture vibrant, fresh and renewed.**

2. Our **Respiratory System renews the body** with fresh air to keep it vibrant. This happens because **red blood cells pick up oxygen in the lungs and carry it to all other cells of the body to re-new its life force.**

3. Ministry of Arts and Culture is patterned after the Respiratory System.

We breathe in fresh air and expel old air. Likewise, arts/cultural centers are places to exchange old ideas for fresh ideas.

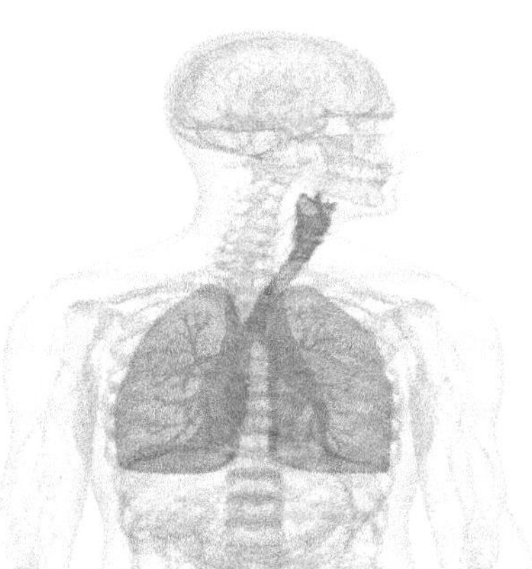

What policy recommendations will help the Ministry of Arts and Culture to fulfill its functionality to assure society is renewed with fresh and clean ideas via re-creational centers as the respiration system does for the human body?

1. <u>**The Ministry of Information**</u> **is any organized system for the collection, organization, storage and communication of information to deliver a product.** IT libraries constantly update to deliver information.

2. Our <u>**Reproductive System**</u> **is a collection of DNA in both sperm and egg**. DNA converge updated volumes of information (super consciousness), at high speeds, to develop systems and networks of information **that will deliver a human being**.

3. The Ministry of Information is patterned after the Reproductive System.

Both store and organize volumes of information to deliver a product.

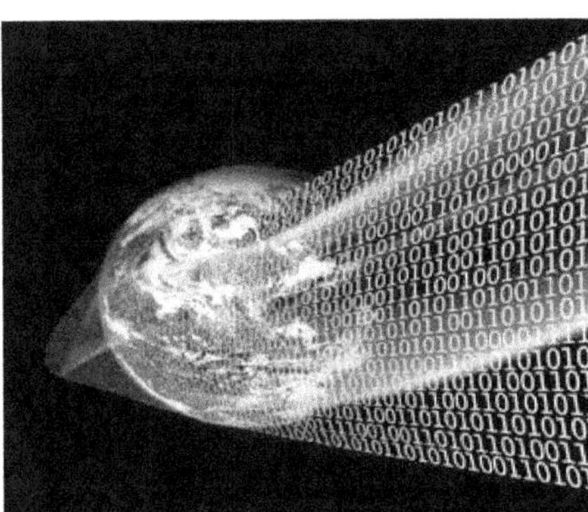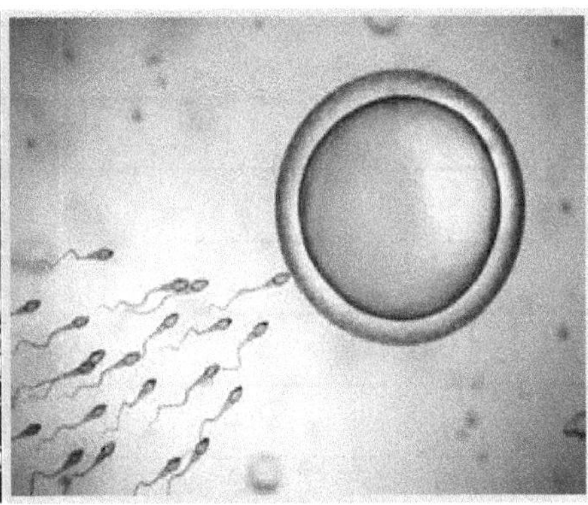

What policy recommendations will help the Ministry of Information to fulfill its functionality to assure the true history of our community/nation is passed on from generation to generation for the world to read and see as does the reproductive system does for human delivery?

____

____

____

____

____

1. **The <u>Ministry of Health and Human Services</u> is a network** of health care providers **that receive information about the community's public health environment**. Health Care systems constantly update records **to remedy public dis-eases**. This means multiple departments and services at work rendering solutions.

2. **Our <u>Nervous System</u>** is a network of sensory organs **receiving information throughout the entire body**. It consists of multiple components constantly being updated to remedy bodily dis-eases, including chronic mental pains.

3. The Ministry of Health and Human Services is the outgrowth and functionality of the Nervous System. Both fuse directly into the Brain or the entire body-politic to maintain stability.

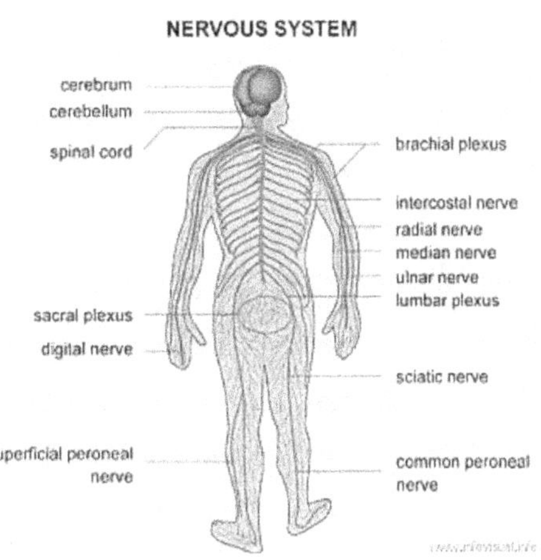

What policy recommendations will help the Ministry of Health and Human Services to fulfill its functionality to assure our entire community receives health care to heal from sorrowful diseased bodily organs as the nervous system does for the entire human body?

1. **The <u>Ministry of Agriculture</u>** is the bases of economics and communal life. The most ancient financial systems were based upon agriculture. It **produces the fertilizer to grow and sustain food production**. Civilization without agri-business is like man/woman without an endocrine system.

2. **Our <u>Endocrine System</u>** is made up of a group of glands that manage and **produce hormones to sustain life**. Hormones represent fertilizer for our organs to assure reproduction and growth.

3. The Ministry of Agriculture is patterned after the Endocrine System. Both produce the substance to grow the means by which our body, community and economy evolves.

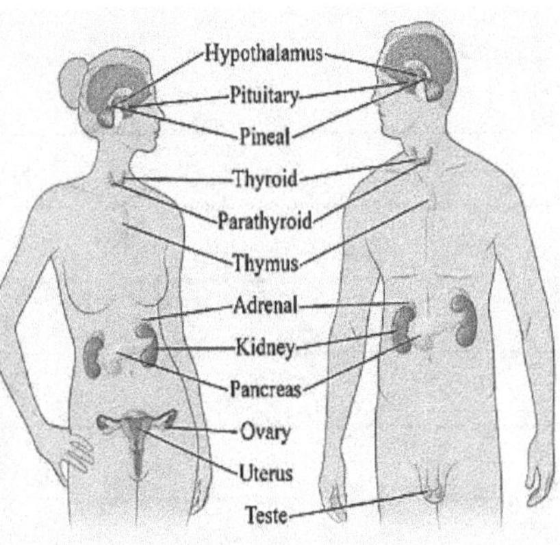

What policy recommendations will help the Ministry of Agriculture to fulfill its functionality to assure land is sustainable to produce food and other agri-business growth as the endocrine system does for the human body.

____

____

____

____

____

Mixed-Use Development Rendering

What is a Mixed-Use Development Community? Provide several cost factors to build one? What harm do we suffer to build a community without social structural policies, moral values and civic participation? Name 5 personal values and 1 skills you can add to make a better community**?**

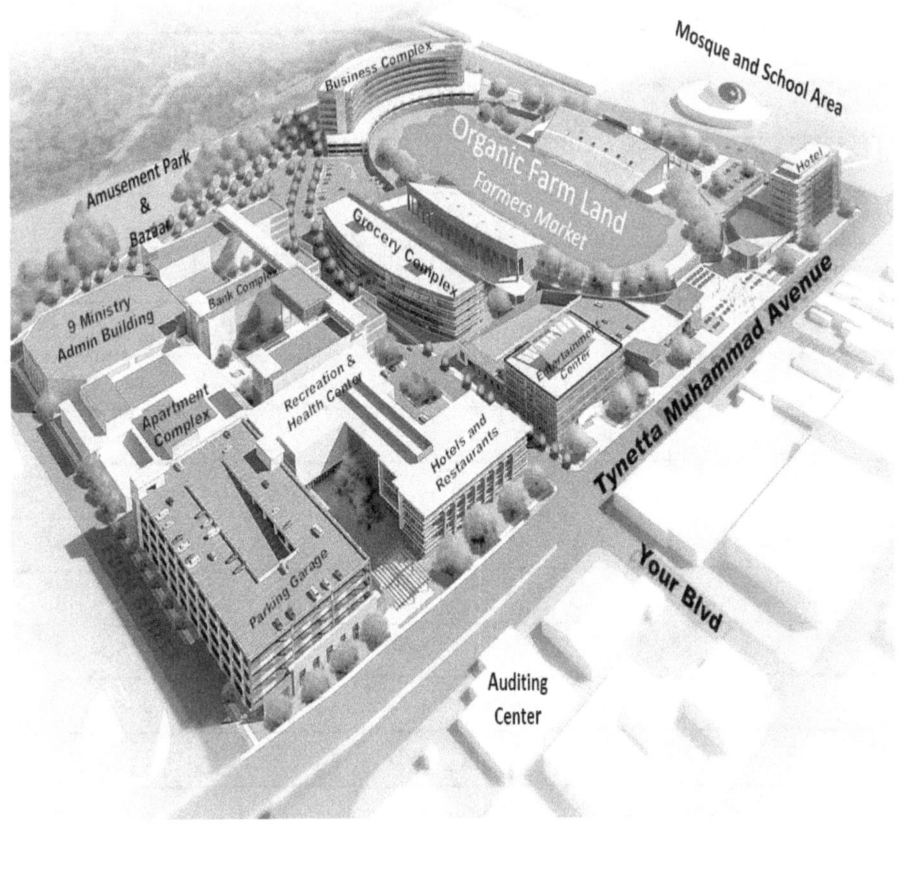

Failed State

A **failed state** is a political body that has disintegrated to a point where basic conditions and responsibilities of a sovereign government no longer function properly. Likewise, when a nation weakens and its standard of living declines, it introduces the possibility of total governmental collapse. The Fund for Peace characterizes a failed state as having the following characteristics:

- Loss of control of its territory, or of the monopoly on the legitimate use of physical force therein
- Erosion of legitimate authority to make collective decisions
- Inability to provide public services
- Inability to interact with other states as a full member of the international community

Common characteristics of a failing state include a central government so weak or ineffective that it has an inability to raise taxes or other support, and has little practical control over much of its territory and hence there is a non-provision of public services. When this happens, widespread corruption and criminality, the intervention of non-state actors, the appearance of refugees and the involuntary movement of populations, and sharp economic decline can occur.[4]

Has Black America, Africa, India or South American citizens suffered from some of the symptoms of a "Failed State"? Explain how and define the meaning of Interregnum in terms of its whys and wherefores?

____

____

____

____

[4] https://en.wikipedia.org/wiki/Failed_state

A
Torchlight
for
America
MINISTER
LOUIS
FARRAKHAN

Your Brain and
9 Systems
-Is Physio Economics-
Knowledge of God-Self
Volume 1
Respiratory
Brain
Skeletal
Reproductive
Muscular
Circulatory
Nervous
Digestive
Immune
Endocrine
3rd Revised Edition
Abdul Wahid Muhammad
Rasheed L Muhammad

10 SYSTEMS OF
THE HUMAN BODY:
A STUDY OF GOVERNMENT
A NEW EDUCATION PARADIGM SEMINAR
CONDUCTED BY: ABDUL WAHID MUHAMMAD & RASHEED L MUHAMMAD
Contact study10systems@gmail.com